365 Stoic Quotes

Daily stoic meditations on virtue, self-control, discipline, wisdom, justice, courage, and moderation

ABSTRACT PRESS

ABSTRACT PRESS

First published in this edition 2021

ISBN-13: 9798727060988

365 Stoic Quotes

Daily stoic meditations on virtue, self-control, discipline, wisdom, justice, courage, and moderation

1

If you want to improve, be content to be thought foolish and stupid.

Epictetus

2

Let us prepare our minds as if we'd come to the very end of life. Let us postpone nothing. Let us balance life's books each day... The one who puts the finishing touches on their life each day is never short of time.

Marcus Aurelius

3

Man conquers the world by conquering himself.

Zeno of Citium

It does not matter what you bear, but how you bear it.

Seneca

Life's three best teachers: heartbreak, empty pocket, failures."

Haemin Sunim

A wise man is superior to any insults which can be put upon him, and the best reply to unseemly behaviour is patience and moderation.

Molière

7

Stop trying to impress others with your stuff and start trying to impress them with your life.

Joshua Becker

8

Anyone who enjoys inner peace is no more broken by failure than he is inflated by success.

Matthieu Ricard

9

Living virtuously is equal to living in accordance with one's experience of the actual course of nature.

Chrysippus

10

A single day among the learned lasts longer than the longest life of the ignorant.

Posidonius

11

Be disentangled from all perceptions. They are not you.

Brian Thompson

12

Neither seek nor avoid, take what comes.

Swami Vivekananda

13

That man lives badly who does not know how to die well.

Seneca

14

Waste no more time arguing what a good man should be.

Marcus Aurelius

15

He who does not desire or fear the uncertain day or capricious fate, is equal to the gods above and loftier than mortals.

Justus Lipsius

16

No man is good by chance. Virtue is something which must be learned.

Seneca

17

The truth is that our finest moments are most likely to occur when we are feeling deeply uncomfortable, unhappy, or unfulfilled. For it is only in such moments, propelled by our discomfort, that we are likely to step out of our ruts and start searching for different ways or truer answers.

M. Scott Peck

18

Events in life mean nothing if you do not reflect on them in a deep way, and ideas from books are pointless if they have no application to life as you live it.

Robert Greene

19

You are a little soul carrying around a corpse.

Epictetus

20

The willing are led by fate, the reluctant dragged.

Cleanthes

21

Others have been in poor health from overindulgence and high living, before exile has provided strength, forcing them to live a more vigorous life.

Musonius Rufus

22

What we desire makes us vulnerable.

Ryan Holiday

23

Don't be the person that looks at the weather report the night before to decide what you are going to do the next day.

David Goggins

24

A bad feeling is a commotion of the mind repugnant to reason, and against nature.

Zeno of Citium

25

Stoicism, understood properly, is a cure for a disease. The disease in question is the anxiety, grief, fear, and various other negative emotions that plague humans and prevent them from experiencing a joyful existence.

William B. Irvine

26

Order your soul. Reduce your wants.

Augustine of Hippo

27

This is my secret. I don't mind what happens.

Jiddu Krishnamurti

28

Happiness is a choice. Forgiveness is a choice.
Acceptance, anger, desire, love... all choices. Your
time. Your choice.

Scott Shaw

29

Uncertainty is an uncomfortable position. But
certainty is an absurd one.

Voltaire

30

It's time you realized that you have something in you more powerful and miraculous than the things that affect you and make you dance like a puppet.

Marcus Aurelius

31

Associate with people who are likely to improve you. Welcome those who you are capable of improving. The process is a mutual one: men learn as they teach.

Seneca

32

Sometimes in life we must fight not only without fear, but also without hope

Alessandro Pertini

33

That which exercises reason is more excellent than that which does not exercise reason; there is nothing more excellent than the universe, therefore the universe exercises reason.

Zeno of Citium

34

The life of men, who pass their time in the midst of affairs, and who wish to be helpful to themselves and to others, is exposed to constant and almost daily troubles and sudden dangers. To guard against and avoid these one needs a mind that is always ready and alert, such as the athletes have who are called "pancratists".

Panaetius

35

In your actions, don't procrastinate. In your conversations, don't confuse. In your thoughts, don't wander. In your soul, don't be passive or aggressive. In your life, don't be all about business.

Marcus Aurelius

Where you arrive does not matter as much as what sort of person you are when you arrive there.

Seneca

A Stoic is someone who transforms fear into prudence, pain into transformation, mistakes into initiation, and desire into undertaking.

Nassim Nicholas Taleb

38

Imagine smiling after a slap in the face. Then think of doing it twenty-four hours a day.

Markus Zusak

39

You are indeed a man of sorrows and have suffered much...pray be seated now, here on this chair, and let us leave our sorrows, bitter though they are, locked up in our own hearts, for weeping is cold comfort and does little good.

Homer

40

The mind that is anxious about future events is miserable.

Seneca

41

The more time you spend in your discomfort zone, the more your comfort zone will expand.

Robin Sharma

42

He who fears death has already lost the life he covets.

Cato the Elder

43

Every hour focus your mind attentively...on the performance of the task in hand, with dignity, human sympathy, benevolence and freedom, and leave aside all other thoughts. You will achieve this, if you perform each action as if it were your last.

Marcus Aurelius

44

Nothing, to my way of thinking, is a better proof of a well ordered mind than a man's ability to stop just where he is and pass some time in his own company.

Seneca

45

How long are you going to wait before you demand the best for yourself?

Epictetus

46

Never let people who choose the path of least resistance steer you away from your chosen path of most resistance.

David Goggins

47

I myself think that the wise man meddles little or not at all in affairs and does his own things.

Chrysippus

48

The vast majority of people make complaining seem to be a basic human need.

Mokokoma Mokhonoana

49

One of the first lessons from Stoicism, then, is to focus our attention and efforts where we have the most power and then let the universe run as it will. This will save us both a lot of energy and a lot of worry.

Massimo Pigliucci

50

People are always looking for shortcuts. The only way to achieve greatness in life is to have patience, consistency, and discipline.

David Goggins

51

Disturbance comes only from within- from our own perceptions. Everything you see will soon alter and cease to exist.

Marcus Aurelius

52

We should not, like sheep, follow the herd of creatures in front of us, making our way where others go, not where we ought to go.

Seneca

53

If you are pained by any external tiling, it is not this things that disturbs you, but your own judgment about it. And it is in your power to wipe out this judgment now.

Jonas Salzgeber

54

External thinks are not the problem. It's your assessment of them. Which you can erase right now.

Marcus Aurelius

55

Missing a train is only painful if you run after it! Likewise, not matching the idea of success others expect from you is only painful if that's what you are seeking.

Nassim Nicholas Taleb

56

The happiness of your life depends upon the quality of your thoughts.

Marcus Aurelius

57

A wise man never loses anything if he has himself.

Michel de Montaigne

58

There are two of the most immediately useful thoughts you will dip into. First that things cannot touch the mind: they are external and inert; anxieties can only come from your internal judgement. Second, that all these things you see will change almost as you look at them, and then will be no more. Constantly bring to mind all that you yourself have already seen changed. The universe is change: life is judgement.

Marcus Aurelius

Virtue is the health of the soul.

Aristo of Chios

The robbed that smiles steals something from the thief.

Othello

Well-being is attained little by little, and nevertheless is no little thing itself.

Zeno of Citium

62

Pay attention to your enemies, for they are the first to discover your mistakes.

Antisthenes

When you transform your mind, everything you experience is transformed.

Mingyur Rinpoche

Zoom out. In the grand scheme of things, is this really going to affect you? We can't even remember what we were doing 5 days ago, let alone five years. What matters is how you feel now. If it makes you upset, let it go. If it feels good, let it consume you.

Thibaut

Remember that your perception of the world is a reflection of your state of consciousness.

Eckhart Tolle

If a man can reduce his needs to zero, he is truly free: there is nothing that can be taken from him; nothing can hurt him.

John Boyd

67

That one wants nothing to be different, not forward, not backwards, not in all eternity. Not merely bear what is necessary, still less conceal it... but love it.

Friedrich Nietzsche

And here you may mention anything you care to name — a fit of uninterrupted coughing to violent that it brings up part of the internal organs, having one's very entrails seared by a fever, thirst, having limbs wrenched in different directions with dislocations of the joints... There have been men who have undergone these experiences and never uttered a groan.

Seneca

To accept injury without a spirit of savage resentment-to show ourselves merciful toward those who wrong us-being a source of good hope to them-is characteristic of a benevolent and civilized way of life.

Musonius Rufus

70

Define for me now what the "indifferents" are. Whatever things we cannot control. Tell me the upshot. They are nothing to me.

Epictetus

71

Adopt the pace of nature: her secret is patience.

Ralph Waldo Emerson

72

Change: nothing inherently bad in the process, nothing inherently good in the result.

Marcus Aurelius

73

Set aside a certain number of days during which you shall be content with the scantiest and cheapest fare, with coarse and rough dress, saying to yourself the while, "Is this the condition that I feared?"

Seneca

74

Run down the list of those who felt intense anger at something: the most famous, the most unfortunate, the most hated, the most whatever: Where is all that now? Smoke, dust, legend...or not even a legend. Think of all the examples. And how trivial the things we want so passionately are.

Marcus Aurelius

75

You cannot overestimate the unimportance of practically everything.

Greg McKeown

76

The ultimate power in life is to be completely self-reliant, completely yourself.

Robert Greene

77

Being a stoic does not mean being a robot. Being a stoic means remaining calm both at the height of pleasure and the depths of misery.

Abhijit Naskar

78

The best livelihood, particularly for the strong, is earning a living from the soil, whether you own your land or not. Many can support their families by farming land owned by the state or private landowners. Some even get rich through hard work with their own hands. The earth repays those who cultivate her, both justly and well, multiplying what she received – endowing in abundance all the necessities of life to anyone willing to work-and all this without violating your dignity or self-respect!

Musonius Rufus

79

Ensure you endure.

Maxime Lagacé

80

Never call yourself a philosopher, nor talk a great deal among the unlearned about theorems, but act conformably to them. Thus, at an entertainment, don't talk how persons ought to eat, but eat as you ought. For remember that in this manner Socrates also universally avoided all ostentation. And when persons came to him and desired to be recommended by him to philosophers, he took and recommended them, so well did he bear being overlooked. So that if ever any talk should happen among the unlearned concerning philosophic theorems, be you, for the most part, silent. For there is great danger in immediately throwing out what you have not digested. And, if anyone tells you that you know nothing, and you are not nettled at it, then you may be sure that you have begun your business. For sheep don't throw up the grass to show the shepherds how much they have eaten; but, inwardly digesting their food, they outwardly produce wool and milk. Thus, therefore, do you likewise not show theorems to the unlearned, but the actions produced by them after they have been digested.

Epictetus

81

Things which bestow upon the soul no greatness or confidence or freedom from care are not goods. But riches and health and similar conditions do none of these things; therefore, riches and health are not goods. Things which bestow upon the soul no greatness or confidence or freedom from care, but on the other hand create in it arrogance, vanity, and insolence, are evils. But things which are the gift of Fortune drive us into these evil ways. Therefore these things are not goods.

Posidonius

82

You are scared of dying —And tell me, is the kind of life you lead really any different than being dead?

Seneca

83

Between stimulus and response, there is a space. In that space is our power to choose our response.

Viktor Frankl

84

Failure and deprivation are the best educators and purifiers.

Albert Einstein

85

A man is as unhappy as he has convinced himself he is.

Seneca

86

Promise yourself to be so strong that nothing can disturb your peace of mind.

Christian D. Larson

87

Progress daily in your own uncertainty. Live in awareness of the questions.

Bremer Acosta

Desire is a contract that you make with yourself to be unhappy until you get what you want.

Naval Ravikant

Success is based off of your willingness to work your ass off no matter what obstacles are in your way.

David Goggins

Why should we pay so much attention to what the majority thinks?

Socrates

No human thing is of serious importance.

Plato

92

Relentlessly prune bullshit, don't wait to do things that matter, and savour the time you have.

Paul Graham

93

The Fates guide the person who accepts them and hinder the person who resists them.

Cleanthes

94

I am happy because I want nothing from anyone. I do not care for money. Decorations, titles or distinctions mean nothing to me. I do not crave praise. The only thing that gives me pleasure, apart from my work, my violin and my sailboat, is the appreciation of my fellow workers.

Albert Einstein

95

To bear trials with a calm mind robs misfortune of its strength and burden.

Seneca

96

What upsets people is not things themselves, but their judgements about these things.

Epictetus

97

Show people, don't tell people.

David Goggins

98

We cannot control the evil tongues of others; but a good life enables us to disregard them.

Cato the Elder

99

We define ourselves far too often by our past failures. That's not you. You are this person right now. You're the person who has learned from those failures.

Joe Rogan

100

We begin to lose our hesitation to do immoral things when we lose our hesitation to speak of them.

Musonius Rufus

101

The first rule is to keep an untroubled spirit. The second is to look things in the face and know them for what they are.

Marcus Aurelius

102

We will train both soul and body when we accustom ourselves to cold, heat, thirst, hunger, scarcity of food, hardness of bed, abstaining from pleasures, and enduring pains.

Musonius Rufus

103

Do not pray for an easy life, pray for the strength to endure a difficult one.

Bruce Lee

104

Do what you will. Even if you tear yourself apart, most people will continue doing the same things.

Marcus Aurelius

105

The pursuit, even of the best things, ought to be calm and tranquil.

Cicero

106

Life is very short and anxious for those who forget the past, neglect the present, and fear the future.

Seneca

107

Better to endure pain in an honourable manner than to seek joy in a shameful one.

Massimo Pigliucci

108

People are frugal in guarding their personal property; but as soon as it comes to squandering time they are most wasteful of the one thing in which it is right to be stingy.

Seneca

109

The average man is a conformist, accepting miseries and disasters with the stoicism of a cow standing in the rain.

Colin Wilson

110

The limit is not the sky. The limit is the mind.

Wim Hof

111

Happiness is a choice that requires effort at times.

Aeschylus

112

Understand what you can control and what you can't. Forget about the things you can't control and put that energy into the things you can control.

Shane Parrish

113

Won't we, therefore, be willing to endure pain in order to gain complete happiness?

Musonius Rufus

114

Be so busy building your own life that other people's bullshit is of no concern.

Ed Latimore

115

Whatever can happen at any time can happen today.

Seneca

116

Your true self is not your emotion such as anger, frustration or hate. It is the inner witness that knows the rise and fall of your emotion.

Haemin Sunim

117

Until we have begun to go without them, we fail to realize how unnecessary many things are. We've been using them not because we needed them but because we had them.

Seneca

118

What we fear doing most is usually what we most need to do.

Tim Ferris

119

Be tolerant with others and strict with yourself.

Marcus Aurelius

120

Be so busy building your own life that other people's bullshit is of no concern.

Ed Latimore

121

For what does the man who accepts insult do that is wrong? It is the doer of wrong who puts themselves to shame-the sensible man wouldn't go to the law, since he wouldn't even consider that he had been insulted! Besides, to be annoyed or angered about such things would be petty-instead easily and silently bear what has happened, since this is appropriate for those whose purpose is to be noble-minded.

Musonius Rufus

122

Show me one person who cares how they act, someone for whom success is less important than the manner in which it is achieved. While out walking, who gives any thought to the act of walking itself? Who pays attention to the process of planning, not just the outcome?

Epictetus

123

Musonius ordered a thousand sesterces to be given to a man pretending to be a philosopher, when several people told him the man was a bad and vicious fellow, deserving of nothing good, Musonius answered with a smile, 'Well then he deserves money'.

Musonius Rufus

124

Life is so hard; how can we be anything but kind?

Jack Kornfield

125

Those who are serious in ridiculous matters will be ridiculous in serious matters.

Cato the Elder

126

The goal of life is living in agreement with Nature.

Zeno of Citium

127

Everyone faces up more bravely to a thing for which he has long prepared himself, sufferings, even, being withstood if they have been trained for in advance. Those who are unprepared, on the other hand, are panic-stricken by the most insignificant happenings.

Seneca

128

When the world pushes you to your knees, you're in the perfect position to pray.

Rumi

129

Take a deep breath. Get present in the moment and ask yourself what is important this very second.

Greg McKeown

130

Death is not an evil. What is it then? The one law mankind has that is free of all discrimination.

Seneca

131

A fit body, a calm mind, a house full of love. These things cannot be bought — they must be earned.

Naval Ravikant

132

Fear is a natural reaction to moving closer to the truth.

Pema Chödrön

133

How does it help...to make troubles heavier by bemoaning them?

Seneca

134

And this should be one of the primary objectives of philosophy: to reveal to us our shortcomings so we can overcome them and thereby live a good life.

Musonius Rufus

135

The whole future lies in uncertainty: live immediately.

Seneca

136

What do I have? My mind and my body: both of these will fail me given enough time. But while my mind is sharp, I can direct my intention, and while my body is able it can take action. But in both of things I can only have influence and never control, so I must focus my influence in the direction of reason and virtue.

Jett Parker-Holland

137

We're not really here that long, and we don't really matter that much. Nothing that we do lasts. Eventually, you will fade. Your works will fade. Your children will fade. Your thoughts will fade. These planets will fade. This sun will fade. It will all be gone.

Naval Ravikant

138

Some things are in our control and others not. Things in our control are opinion, pursuit, desire, aversion, and, in a word, whatever are our own actions.

Things not in our control are body, property, reputation, command, and, in one word, whatever are not our actions. The things in our control are by nature free, unrestrained, unhindered; but those not in our control are weak, slavish, restrained, belonging to others. Remember, then, that if you suppose that things which are slavish by nature are also free, and that what belongs to others is your own, then you will be hindered. You will lament, you will be disturbed, and you will find fault both with gods and men. But if you suppose that only to be your own which is your own, and what belongs to others such as it really is, then no one will ever compel you or restrain you. Further, you will find fault with no one or accuse no one. You will do nothing against your will. No one will hurt you, you will have no enemies, and you not be harmed.

Epictetus

Everything can be taken from a man but one thing: the last of the human freedoms – to choose one's attitude in any given set of circumstances, to choose one's own way.

Viktor Frankl

140

He who laughs at himself never runs out of things to laugh at.

Epictetus

141

Given that all must die, it is better to die with distinction than to live long.

Musonius Rufus

142

Remind yourself that the past and future are 'indifferent' to you, and that the supreme good, and eudaimonia, can only exist within you, right now, in the present moment.

Donald J. Robertson

143

We are more often frightened than hurt; and we suffer more in imagination than in reality.

Seneca

144

An angry man opens his mouth and shuts his eyes.

Cato the Elder

145

Having the fewest wants, I am nearest to the gods.

Epictetus

146

If you are irritated by every rub, how will your mirror be polished?

Rumi

147

Disgraceful if, in this life where your body does not fail, your soul should fail you first.

Marcus Aurelius

148

True happiness is to enjoy the present, without anxious dependence upon the future, not to amuse ourselves with either hopes or fears but to rest satisfied with what we have, which is sufficient, for he that is so wants nothing. The greatest blessings of mankind are within us and within our reach. A wise man is content with his lot, whatever it may be, without wishing for what he has not.

Seneca

149

Bitter are the roots of study, but how sweet their fruit.

Cato the Elder

150

Expectation is the only seed of disappointment.

Mokokoma Mokhonoana

151

Begin at once to live, and count each separate day as a separate life.

Seneca

152

A man is no bigger than the smallest thing that provokes him.

Dan Horton

153

Luck is what happens when preparation meets opportunity.

Seneca

154

I cannot escape death, but at least I can escape the fear of it.

Epictetus

155

In heaven, everything is good; in hell, everything bad. In the world, since it lies between the two, you find both. We are placed between two extremes, and so participate in both. Good and bad luck alternate; not all is happy, nor all hostile. This world is a zero: on its own, it's worth nothing; joined to heaven, a great deal. Indifference to its variety constitutes good sense - the wise are never surprised. Our life is arranged like a play, everything will be sorted out in the end. Take care, then, to end it well.

Baltasar Gracián

156

In order to protect ourselves we must live like doctors and be continually treating ourselves with reason.

Musonius Rufus

157

The wise man needs nothing and yet he can make good use of anything, whereas the fool 'needs' countless things but can make good use of none of them.

Donald J. Robertson

158

Your existence, my existence is just infinitesimal. It's like a firefly blinking once in the night.

Naval Ravikant

159

You're never given more pain than you can handle.

Byron Katie

160

Stop drifting...Sprint to the finish. Write off your hopes, and if your well-being matters to you, be your own saviour while you can.

Marcus Aurelius

161

Things you won't say on your deathbed: "I wish I paid more attention to what other people think.

Johnny Uzan

162

No amount of anxiety makes any difference to anything that is going to happen.

Alan Watts

163

Drop your concepts, drop your opinions, drop your prejudices, drop your judgments, and you will see that

Anthony de Mello

164

It is not the man who has too little, but the man who craves more, that is poor.

Seneca

165

What then is that which is able to conduct a man? One thing and only one, philosophy. But this consists in keeping the daemon within a man free from violence and unharmed, superior to pains and pleasures, doing nothing without purpose, nor yet falsely and with hypocrisy, not feeling the need of another man's doing or not doing anything; and besides, accepting all that happens, and all that is allotted, as coming from thence, wherever it is, from whence he himself came; and, finally, waiting for death with a cheerful mind, as being nothing else than a dissolution of the elements of which every living being is compounded. But if there is no harm to the elements themselves in each continually changing into another, why should a man have any apprehension about the change and dissolution of all the elements? For it is according to nature, and nothing is evil which is according to nature.

Marcus Aurelius

166

The more you seek the uncomfortable, the more you will become comfortable.

Conor McGregor

167

Some of the best things that have ever happened to us wouldn't have happened to us, if it weren't for some of the worst things that have ever happened to us.

Mokokoma Mokhonoana

168

You act like mortals in all that you fear, and like immortals in all that you desire.

Seneca

169

You need patience, discipline, and an agility to take losses and adversity without going crazy.

Charlie Munger

170

When the longest- and shortest-lived of us dies, their loss is precisely equal. For the sole thing of which any of us can be deprived is the present, since this is all we own, and nobody can lose what is not theirs.

Marcus Aurelius

171

Buy not what you want, but what you have need of; what you do not want is dear at a farthing.

Cato the Elder

172

If you lose self-control everything will fall.

John Wooden

173

The key is to keep company only with people who uplift you, whose presence calls forth your best.

Epictetus

174

If we were to measure what is good by how much pleasure it brings, nothing would be better than self-control- if we were to measure what is to be avoided by its pain, nothing would be more painful than lack of self-control.

Musonius Rufus

175

Nature gave us reason, in order that it might survey everything else, and, together with all things, or rather prior to all things, might direct its attention to Nature herself.

Hierocles

176

There is a correlation between how seriously we take life and how many problems it gives us.

Mokokoma Mokhonoana

177

Don't grieve. Anything you lose comes around in another form.

Rumi

178

You may leave this life at any moment: have this possibility in your mind in all that you do or say or think.

Marcus Aurelius

179

The end may be defined as life in accordance with nature or, in other words, in accordance with our own human nature as well as that of the universe.

Zeno of Citium

180

Don't seek for everything to happen as you wish it would, but rather wish that everything happens as it actually will—then your life will flow well.

Epictetus

181

What you're supposed to do when you don't like a thing is change it. If you can't change it, change the way you think about it. Don't complain.

Maya Angelou

182

He who has equipped himself for the whole of life does not need to be advised concerning each separate thing, because he is now trained to meet his problem as a whole; for he knows not merely how he should live with his wife or his son, but how he should live aright.

Aristo of Chios

183

A rational person can find peace by cultivating indifference to things outside of their control.

Naval Ravikant

184

If you're going through hell, keep going.

Winston Churchill

185

Men seek out retreats for themselves in the country, by the seaside, on the mountains... nowhere can a man find a retreat more peaceful or more free from trouble than his own soul.

Marcus Aurelius

186

How do you move forward? One step at a time. How do you lose weight? One kilo at a time. How do you write a book? One page at a time. How do you build a relationship? One day at a time. In a world obsessed with speed, never forget things of real worth and value take time.

Thibaut

187

Self-control is strength. Right thought is mastery. Calmness is power.

James Allen

188

It never ceases to amaze me: we all love ourselves more than other people, but care more about their opinion than our own.

Marcus Aurelius

189

If you want to improve, be content to be thought foolish and stupid with regard to external things. Don't wish to be thought to know anything; and even if you appear to be somebody important to others, distrust yourself. For, it is difficult to both keep your faculty of choice in a state conformable to nature, and at the same time acquire external things. But while you are careful about the one, you must of necessity neglect the other.

Epictetus

190

There are two of the most immediately useful thoughts you will dip into. First that things cannot touch the mind: they are external and inert; anxieties can only come from your internal judgement. Second, that all these things you see will change almost as you look at them, and then will be no more. Constantly bring to mind all that you yourself have already seen changed. The universe is change: life is judgement.

Marcus Aurelius

191

Understand: in life as in war, nothing ever happens just as you expect it to.

Robert Greene

192

The universe itself is God and the universal outpouring of its soul.

Chrysippus

193

If you accomplish something good with hard work,
the labour passes quickly, but the good endures; if
you do something shameful in pursuit of pleasure,
the pleasure passes quickly, but the shame endures.

Musonius Rufus

194

There are clearly people for whom Stoicism
immediately 'clicks', it comes natural, and others for
whom it doesn't. Then again, Stoicism isn't the only
positive philosophy of life. Buddhism is an excellent
alternative, if it speaks more clearly to one's
personality or cultural background.

Massimo Pigliucci

195

Everything that happens is either endurable or not. If it's endurable, then endure it. Stop complaining. If it's unendurable… then stop complaining. Your destruction will mean its end as well. Just remember: you can endure anything your mind can make endurable, by treating it as in your interest to do so.

Marcus Aurelius

196

Wealth is able to buy the pleasures of eating, drinking and other sensual pursuits-yet can never afford a cheerful spirit or freedom from sorrow.

Musonius Rufus

197

Man's character is his fate.

Heraclitus

198

What good are gilded rooms or precious stones-fitted on the floor, inlaid in the walls, carried from great distances at the greatest expense? These things are pointless and unnecessary-without them isn't it possible to live healthy? Aren't they the source of constant trouble? Don't they cost vast sums of money that, through public and private charity, may have benefited many?

Musonius Rufus

199

Today I have got myself out of all my perplexities; or rather, I have got my perplexities out of myself, for they were not without, but within; they lay in my own outlook.

Marcus Aurelius

200

To make a goal of comfort or happiness has never appealed to me; a system of ethics built on this basis would be sufficient only for a herd of cattle.

Albert Einstein

201

You could leave life right now. Let that determine what you do and say and think.

Marcus Aurelius

202

You are the sky. Everything else – it's just the weather.

Pema Chödrön

203

If a man knows not which port he sails, no wind is favourable.

Seneca

204

Curb your desire—don't set your heart on so many things and you will get what you need.

Epictetus

205

We are quick to forget that just being alive is an extraordinary piece of good luck, a remote event, a chance occurrence of monstrous proportions.

Nassim Nicholas Taleb

206

You will earn the respect of all if you begin by earning the respect of yourself. Don't expect to encourage good deeds in people conscious of your own misdeeds.

Musonius Rufus

207

The most important reason to live in the moment is nothing lasts forever. Enjoy the moment while it's in front of you. Be present. Accept life for what it is: a finite span of time with infinite possibilities.

Joshua Fields Millburn

208

When someone is properly grounded in life, they shouldn't have to look outside themselves for approval.

Epictetus

209

Happiness isn't outside of us, but actually comes from within.

Leo Babauta

210

The weak can never forgive. Forgiveness is the attribute of the strong.

Mahatma Gandhi

211

It is not so much our friends' help that helps us as the confident knowledge that they will help us.

Epicurus

212

What is death? A scary mask. Take it off – see, it doesn't bite. Eventually, body and soul will have to separate, just as they existed separately before we were born. So why be upset if it happens now? If it isn't now, it's later.

Epictetus

213

As long as you remember that everything is exactly how it's supposed to be, you will always be sane.

Alan Watts

214

If you make happiness your goal, you'll be disappointed. If you make presence your goal, you'll be satisfied.

Maxime Lagacé

215

Patience is the best remedy for every trouble.

Plautus

216

Weak men act to satisfy their needs, stronger men their duties.

Nassim Nicholas Taleb

217

Peace of mind is that mental condition in which you have accepted the worst.

Lin Yutang

218

First say to yourself what you would be; and then do what you have to do.

Epictetus

219

When you pursue wisdom, you will soon realize how much you don't know. Your knowledge will be incomplete, but continually developing through your curiosity. Arrogance blocks new information from coming in. When you're conceited, you'll resist change, and struggle to preserve your fixed image. Don't fall into smug idleness, used to comfort. Challenge what you think you know, not caring if other people see you as a fool. Progress daily in your own uncertainty.

Bremer Acosta

220

Generally speaking, if you devote yourself to the life
of philosophy, whilst tilling the land at the same time,
I couldn't compare it to any other way of life, nor
would I prefer any other livelihood. It is living more
in accord with nature-drawing your sustenance
directly from the earth-the nurse and mother of us all-
rather than from another source.

Musonius Rufus

221

The best revenge is not to be like your enemy.

Marcus Aurelius

222

Remember that you must behave in life as at a dinner party. Is anything brought around to you? Put out your hand and take your share with moderation. Does it pass by you? Don't stop it. Is it not yet come? Don't stretch your desire towards it, but wait till it reaches you. Do this with regard to children, to a wife, to public posts, to riches, and you will eventually be a worthy partner of the feasts of the gods. And if you don't even take the things which are set before you, but are able even to reject them, then you will not only be a partner at the feasts of the gods, but also of their empire.

Epictetus

223

There is no cure for birth and death save to enjoy the interval.

George Santayana

224

I love to go and see all the things I am happy
without.

Socrates

225

Since I say that this is the case, the person who is
practicing to become a philosopher must seek to
overcome himself so that he won't welcome pleasure
and avoid pain, so that he won't love living and fear
death, and so that, in the case of money, he won't
honour receiving over giving.

Musonius Rufus

226

Wise men profit more from fools than fools from
wise men; for the wise men shun the mistakes of
fools, but fools do not imitate the successes of the
wise.

Cato the Elder

227

No person has the power to have everything they want, but it is in their power not to want what they don't have, and to cheerfully put to good use what they do have.

Seneca

228

You have power over your mind — not outside events. Realize this, and you will find strength.

Marcus Aurelius

229

Why do you so earnestly seek the truth in distant places? Look for delusion and truth in the bottom of your own hearts.

Ryókan

230

We humans are unhappy in large part because we are insatiable; after working hard to get what we want, we routinely lose interest in the object of our desire. Rather than feeling satisfied, we feel a bit bored, and in response to this boredom, we go on to form new, even grander desires.

William B. Irvine

231

Anyone can steer the ship when the sea is calm.

Publilius Syrus

232

Control your perceptions. Direct your actions properly. Willingly accept what's outside your control.

Ryan Holiday

233

Patience is the companion of wisdom.

Augustine of Hippo

234

Think of the life you have lived until now as over and, as a dead man, see what's left as a bonus and live it according to Nature. Love the hand that fate deals you and play it as your own, for what could be more fitting?

Marcus Aurelius

235

Growth and comfort do not coexist.

Ginny Rometty

236

As people very often place intrinsic value on things outside of their direct control, and doing so undoubtedly contributes to human suffering in many ways.

Donald J. Robertson

237

You don't suffer because things are impermanent. You suffer because things are impermanent and you think they are permanent.

Thich Nhat Hanh

238

Ignorant men differ from beasts only in their figure.

Cleanthes

239

You can discard most of the junk that clutters your mind — things that exist only there. And you will immediately make vast space for yourself by grasping the whole universe in your thought, by contemplating the eternity of time, and by reflecting on the speed with which things change — each part of everything, the brief gap from birth to death, the infinite time before, and the equally infinite time that follows.

Marcus Aurelius

240

Remind yourself that the past and future are 'indifferent' to you, and that the supreme good, and eudaimonia, can only exist within you, right now, in the present moment.

Donald J. Robertson

241

He who reigns within himself, and rules passions, desires, and fears, is more than a king.

John Milton

242

Is the child or wife of another dead? There is no one who would not say, "This is an accident of mortality." But if anyone's own child happens to die, it is immediately, "Alas! how wretched am I!" It should be always remembered how we are affected on hearing the same thing concerning others.

Epictetus

243

Let a man accept his destiny, No pity and no tears.

Euripides

244

To help us to cheerfully endure those hardships which we may expect to suffer because of virtue and goodness, it is useful to recall what hardships people will endure for immoral reasons. Consider what lustful lovers undergo for the sake of evil desires-and how much exertion others expend for the sake of profit-how much suffering pursuing fame - bear in mind that they all submit to all kinds of toil and hardship voluntarily. It's monstrous that they endure such things for no honourable reward, yet for the sake of the good (not only the avoidance of evil that wrecks our lives-also the gain of virtue) we're not ready to bear the slightest hardship.

Musonius Rufus

245

Others have been plundered, indiscriminately, set upon, betrayed, beaten up, attacked with poison or with calumny — mention anything you like, it has happened to plenty of people.

Seneca

246

When we are no longer able to change a situation,
we are challenged to change ourselves.

Viktor Frankl

247

An arrow can only be shot by pulling it backward.
So when life is dragging you back with difficulties, it
means that it's going to launch you into something
great. So just focus, and keep aiming.

Paulo Coelho

248

Before I became old I tried to live well; now that I
am old, I shall try to die well; but dying well means
dying gladly.

Seneca

249

It takes courage to accept life fully, to say yes to our life, yes to our karma, yes to our mind, emotions and whatever else unfolds.

Dzigar Kongtrul Rinpoche

250

To be even-minded is the greatest virtue.

Heraclitus

251

Now is the time to get serious about living your ideals. How long can you afford to put off who you really want to be? Your nobler self cannot wait any longer. Put your principles into practice now. Stop the excuses and the procrastination. This is your life! Decide to be extraordinary and do what you need to do – now.

Epictetus

252

They lose the day in expectation of the night, and the night in fear of the dawn.

Seneca

253

The obstacle in the path becomes the path. Never forget, within every obstacle is an opportunity to improve our condition.

Ryan Holiday

254

If melodiously piping flutes sprang from the olive, would you doubt that a knowledge of flute-playing resided in the olive? And what if plane trees bore harps which gave forth rhythmical sounds? Clearly you would think in the same way that the art of music was possessed by plane trees. Why, then, seeing that the universe gives birth to beings that are animate and wise, should it not be considered animate and wise itself?

Zeno of Citium

255

We find comfort among those who agree with us –
growth among those who don't.

Frank A. Clark

256

Evil: the same old thing. No matter what happens,
keep this in mind: It's the same old thing, from one
end of the world to the other. It fills the history
books, ancient and modern, and the cities, and the
houses too. Nothing new at all.

Marcus Aurelius

257

The meaning of life is just to be alive. It is so plain
and so obvious and so simple. And yet, everybody
rushes around in a great panic as if it were
necessary to achieve something beyond themselves.

Alan Watts

258

Warriors should suffer their pain silently.

Erin Hunter

259

I begin to speak only when I'm certain what I'll say isn't better left unsaid.

Cato the Younger

260

Say to yourself first thing in the morning: Today I shall meet people who are meddling, ungrateful, aggressive, treacherous, malicious, unsocial. All this has afflicted them through their ignorance of true good and evil. But I have seen that the nature of good is what is right, and the nature of evil is what is wrong; and I have reflected that the nature of the offender himself is akin to my own – not a kinship of blood or seed, but a sharing in the same mind, the same fragment of divinity. Therefore I cannot be harmed by any of them as none will infect me with their wrong. Nor can I be angry with my kinsmen or hate him. We were born for cooperation, like feet, like hands, like eyelids, like the rows of upper and lower teeth. So to work in opposition to one another is against nature: and anger or rejection is opposition

Marcus Aurelius

261

The art of being wise is the art of knowing what to overlook. William James
The art of being wise is the art of knowing what to overlook. William James
The art of being wise is the art of knowing what to overlook. William James
The art of being wise is the art of knowing what to overlook.

William James

262

A gem cannot be polished without friction, nor a man perfected without trials.

Seneca

263

Anger so clouds the mind that it cannot perceive the truth.

Cato the Elder

264

Progress is not achieved by luck or accident, but by working on yourself daily.

Epictetus

265

What is to give light must endure burning.

Viktor Frankl

266

If it is not right, do not do it, if it is not true, do not say it.

Marcus Aurelius

267

It's your road and yours alone. Others may walk it with you, but no one can walk it for you.

Rumi

268

Just that you do the right thing. The rest doesn't matter.

Marcus Aurelius

269

Flee sloth; for the indolence of the soul is the decay of the body.

Cato the Elder

270

Within you, there is a stillness and a sanctuary to which you can retreat at any time and be yourself.

Hermann Hesse

271

He who angers you conquers you.

Elizabeth Kenny

272

A calm and modest life brings more happiness than the pursuit of success combined with constant restlessness.

Albert Einstein

273

Be stoic: Just do the right thing. Just keep going.

Maxime Lagacé

274

I judge you unfortunate because you have never lived through misfortune. You have passed through life without an opponent—no one can ever know what you are capable of, not even you.

Seneca

275

Amor fati – 'Love your fate', which is in fact your life.

Friedrich Nietzsche

276

Remember: you shouldn't be surprised that a fig tree produces figs, nor the world what it produces. A good doctor isn't surprised when his patients have fevers, or a helmsman when the wind blows against him.

Marcus Aurelius

277

Wise people are in want of nothing, and yet need many things. On the other hand, nothing is needed by fools, for they do not understand how to use anything, but are in want of everything.

Chrysippus

278

You can't stop the waves, but you can learn how to surf.

Jon Kabat-Zinn

279

Stoicism teaches how to keep a calm and rational mind no matter what happens to you and it helps you understand and focus on what you can control and not worry about and accept what you can't control.

Jonas Salzgeber

280

Discomfort is a wise teacher.

Caroline Myss

281

Choose not to be harmed — and you won't feel harmed. Don't feel harmed — and you haven't been.

Marcus Aurelius

282

Expect the river to be wild, surprising and challenging. To expect the opposite is to live in delusion.

Maxime Lagacé

283

Death is neither a good nor a bad thing, for that alone which is something can be a good or a bad thing: but that which is nothing, and reduces all things to nothing, does not hand us over to either fortune, because good and bad require some material to work upon. Fortune cannot take a hold of that which Nature has let go, nor can a man be unhappy if he is nothing.

Seneca

284

The great law of nature is that it never stops. There is no end.

Ryan Holiday

285

By contemplating the impermanence of everything in the world, we are forced to recognize that every time we do something could be the last time we do it, and this recognition can invest the things we do with a significance and intensity that would otherwise be absent.

William B. Irvine

286

We should not use philosophy like a herbal remedy, to be discarded when we're through. Rather, we must allow philosophy to remain with us, continually guarding our judgements throughout life, forming part of our daily regimen, like eating a nutritious diet or taking physical exercise.

Musonius Rufus

287

Give yourself fully to your endeavours. Decide to construct your character through excellent actions and determine to pay the price of a worthy goal. The trials you encounter will introduce you to your strengths.

Epictetus

288

Not even once has life or the weather complained about a human being.

Mokokoma Mokhonoana

289

To accuse others for one's own misfortune is a sign of want of education. To accuse oneself shows that one's education has begun. To accuse neither oneself nor others shows that one's education is complete.

Epictetus

290

Self-control is the chief element in self-respect, and self-respect is the chief element in courage.

Thucydides

291

I've gotten a lot of comfort from the philosophy of the Roman Stoics. For me, one of the most powerful ideas of Stoicism is that you can't pick or choose in the world what you want to happen and what you don't want to happen, and that actually if you did get to choose, the version you would come up with would be unsociable, lame, and basically less beautiful than the truth.

Elif Batuman

292

Remember this: the pain is all in your head.

Ray Dalio

293

Just keep in mind: the more we value things outside our control, the less control we have.

Epictetus

294

It is not daily increase but daily decrease, hack away the unessential. The closer to the source, the less wastage there is.

Bruce Lee

295

This is our big mistake: to think we look forward to death. Most of death is already gone. Whatever time has passed is owned by death.

Seneca

296

In life, it doesn't matter what happens to you or where you came from. It matters what you do with what happens and what you've been given.

Ryan Holiday

297

He who is running a race ought to endeavour and strive to the utmost of his ability to come off victor; but it is utterly wrong for him to trip up his competitor, or to push him aside. So in life it is not unfair for one to seek for himself what may accrue to his benefit; but it is not right to take it from another.

Chrysippus

298

All greatness comes from suffering.

Naval Ravikant

299

If you are ruled by mind you are a king, if by body,
a slave.

Cato the Elder

300

Take a lyre player: he's relaxed when he performs
alone, but put him in front of an audience, and it's a
different story, no matter how beautiful his voice or
how well he plays the instrument. Why? Because he
not only wants to perform well, he wants to be well
received — and the latter lies outside his control.

Epictetus

301

Nothing external to you has any power over you.

Ralph Waldo Emerson

302

Great times are great softeners.

Ryan Holiday

303

No evil is honourable: but death is honourable; therefore death is not evil.

Zeno of Citium

304

If anyone can refute me—show me I'm making a mistake or looking at things from the wrong perspective—I'll gladly change. It's the truth I'm after, and the truth never harmed anyone.

Marcus Aurelius

305

That's why the philosophers warn us not to be satisfied with mere learning, but to add practice and then training. For as time passes we forget what we learned and end up doing the opposite, and hold opinions the opposite of what we should.

Epictetus

306

He who fears death will never do anything worth of a man who is alive.

Seneca

307

All things are parts of one single system, which is called nature; the individual life is good when it is in harmony with nature.

Zeno of Citium

308

If anyone tells you that a certain person speaks ill of you, do not make excuses about what is said of you but answer, "He was ignorant of my other faults, else he would have not mentioned these alone."

Epictetus

309

The cucumber is bitter? Then throw it out. There are brambles in the path? Then go around them. That's all you need to know. Nothing more. Don't demand to know "why such things exist." Anyone who understands the world will laugh at you, just as a carpenter would if you seemed shocked at finding sawdust in his workshop, or a shoemaker at scraps of leather left over from work.

Marcus Aurelius

310

A man who is a master of patience is master of everything else.

George Savile

311

Wealth consists not in having great possessions, but in having few wants.

Epictetus

312

Effortless stoicism will come when you have dismantled everything in your mind that produces reactions.

James Pierce

313

To lose patience is to lose the battle.

Mahatma Gandhi

314

Riches are a cause of evil, not because, of themselves, they do any evil, but because they goad men on so that they are ready to do evil.

Posidonius

315

Be true to whoever or whatever you are and wear it like a badge of honour. Fit in with one person and one person only: yourself.

David Goggins

316

The mind of someone listening to a philosopher, if the things said are useful, helpful and furnish remedies for faults and errors, has no leisure and time for profuse and extravagant praise. ... Great applause and admiration are not unrelated, but the greatest admiration yields silence rather than words.

Musonius Rufus

317

To be stoic is not to be emotionless, but to remain unaffected by your emotions.

James Pierce

318

True happiness is to enjoy the present, without anxious dependence upon the future, not to amuse ourselves with either hopes or fears but to rest satisfied with what we have, which is sufficient, for he that is so wants nothing.

Seneca

319

If it's endurable, then endure it. Stop complaining.

Marcus Aurelius

320

He is a wise man who does not grieve for the things which he has not, but rejoices for those which he has.

Epictetus

321

The basic philosophy of stoicism is that you have nothing real external to your own consciousness, that the only thing real is in fact your consciousness.

Roger Avary

322

I have to die. If it is now, well then I die now; if later, then now I will take my lunch, since the hour for lunch has arrived – and dying I will tend to later.

Epictetus

323

The wise man is neither raised up by prosperity nor cast down by adversity; for always he has striven to rely predominantly on himself, and to derive all joy from himself.

Seneca

324

Stoicism is about the domestication of emotions, not their elimination.

Nassim Nicholas Taleb

325

All the good are friends of one another.

Zeno of Citium

326

It can ruin your life only if it ruins your character. Otherwise it cannot harm you — inside or out.

Marcus Aurelius

327

Discomfort is the currency of success.

Brooke Castillo

328

To complain is always nonacceptance of what is.

Eckhart Tolle

329

What man actually needs is not a tensionless state but rather the striving and struggling for some goal worthy of him.

Viktor Frankl

330

It does not matter what you bear, but how you bear it.

Seneca

331

When a dog is tied to a cart, if it wants to follow, it is pulled and follows, making its spontaneous act coincide with necessity. But if the dog does not follow, it will be compelled in any case. So it is with men too: even if they don't want to, they will be compelled to follow what is destined.

Zeno of Citium

332

There could be no justice, unless there were also injustice; no courage, unless there were cowardice; no truth, unless there were falsehood.

Chrysippus

333

Difficulty shows what men are. Therefore when a difficulty falls upon you, remember that God, like a trainer of wrestlers, has matched you with a rough young man. Why? So that you may become an Olympic conqueror; but it is not accomplished without sweat.

Epictetus

334

Too many people believe that everything must be pleasurable in life.

Robert Greene

335

Get it into your head once and for all, my simple and very fainthearted fellow, that what fools call humanness is nothing but a weakness born of fear and egoism; that this chimerical virtue, enslaving only weak men, is unknown to those whose character is formed by stoicism.

Marquis de Sade

336

To enjoy the rainbow first enjoy the rain.

Paulo Coelho

337

It is more necessary for the soul to be cured than the body; for it is better to die than to live badly.

Epictetus

338

Many men will meet me who are drunkards, lustful, ungrateful, greedy, and excited by the frenzy of ambition.

Seneca

339

The things you own end up owning you.

Joshua Fields Millburn

340

For are not even savage animals, and such as are naturally most hostile to our race, and who are taken away by violence, and at first are detained by chains, and confined in iron cages, are rot these afterwards rendered mild by a certain mode of treatment, and by daily supplying them with food? And will not the man who is a brother, or even any casual person, who deserves attention in a much greater degree than a brute, be changed to milder manners by proper treatment, though he should not entirely forsake his rusticity? In our behaviour, therefore, towards every man, and in a much greater degree towards a brother, we should imitate the reply of Socrates to one who said to him, "May I die unless I am revenged on you." For his answer was, 'May I die, if I do not make you my friend.'

Hierocles

341

It is easier to find men who will volunteer to die, than to find those who are willing to endure pain with patience.

Julius Ceasar

342

Self-discipline and self-control determine the quality of your life more than anything else.

Ed Latimore

343

Hang on to your youthful enthusiasms — you'll be able to use them better when you're older.

Seneca

344

Life is a shipwreck, but we must not forget to sing in the lifeboats.

Voltaire

345

Never depend on the admiration of others. There is no strength in it. Personal merit cannot be derived from an external source. It is not to be found in your personal associations, nor can it be found in the regard of other people. It is a fact of life that other people, even people who love you, will not necessarily agree with your ideas, understand you, or share your enthusiasms. Grow up! Who cares what other people think about you!

Epictetus

346

Nothing ever goes away until it has taught us what we need to know.

Pema Chödrön

347

It's something like going on an ocean voyage. What can I do? Pick the captain, the boat, the date, and the best time to sail. But then a storm hits... What are my options? I do the only thing I am in a position to do, drown — but fearlessly, without bawling or crying out to God, because I know that what is born must also die.

Epictetus

348

Choose to die well while you can; wait too long, and it might become impossible to do so.

Musonius Rufus

349

I laugh at those who think they can damage me. They do not know who I am, they do not know what I think, they cannot even touch the things which are really mine and with which I live.

Epictetus

350

Stoicism is the wisdom of madness and cynicism the madness of wisdom.

Bergen Evans

351

Someone despises me? That is his concern. But I will see to it that I am not found guilty of any word or action deserving contempt. Will he hate me? This is his concern. But I will be kind and well-intentioned to all, and ready to show this very person what he is failing to see – not in any criticism or display of tolerance, but with genuine good will, like the famous Phocion. This should the quality of our inner thoughts, which are open to the god's eyes: they should see a man not disposed to any complaint and free of self-pity. And what harm can you suffer, if you yourself at this present moment are acting in kind with your own nature and accepting what suits the present purpose of universal nature – a man at full stretch for the achievement, this way or that, of the common good?

Marcus Aurelius

352

Difficulty is what wakes up the genius.

Nassim Nicholas Taleb

353

While we wait for life, life passes.

Seneca

354

We love being mentally strong, but we hate situations that allow us to put our mental strength to good use.

Mokokoma Mokhonoana

355

He has the most who is content with the least.

Diogenes

356

Problems only exist in the human mind.

Anthony de Mello

357

There are never any occasions when you need think yourself safe because you wield the weapons of Fortune: Fight with your own! Fortune does not furnish arms against herself; hence men equipped against their foes are unarmed against Fortune herself.

Posidonius

Learn to be indifferent to what makes no difference.

Marcus Aurelius

The worst ruler is one who cannot rule himself.

Cato the Elder

360

Come what may, all bad fortune is to be conquered by endurance.

Virgil

361

Death is a release from and an end of all pains: beyond it our sufferings cannot extend: it restores us to the peaceful rest in which we lay before we were born. If anyone pities the dead, he ought also to pity those who have not been born. Death is neither a good nor a bad thing, for that alone which is something can be a good or a bad thing: but that which is nothing, and reduces all things to nothing, does not hand us over to either fortune, because good and bad require some material to work upon. Fortune cannot take a hold of that which Nature has let go, nor can a man be unhappy if he is nothing.

Seneca

362

The chief task in life is simply this: to identify and separate matters so that I can say clearly to myself which are externals not under my control, and which have to do with the choices I actually control. Where then do I look for good and evil? Not to uncontrollable externals, but within myself to the choices that are my own.

Epictetus

363

At any given moment, you can choose to follow the chain of thoughts, emotions, and sensations that reinforce a perception of yourself as vulnerable and limited, or to remember that your true nature is pure, unconditioned, and incapable of being harmed.

Mingyur Rinpoche

364

Nothing endures but change.

Heraclitus

365

What upsets people is not things themselves but their judgments about the things. For example, death is nothing dreadful (or else it would have appeared dreadful to Socrates), but instead the judgment about death that it is dreadful—that is what is dreadful. So, when we are thwarted or upset or distressed, let us never blame someone else but rather ourselves, that is, our own judgments. An uneducated person accuses others when he is doing badly; a partly educated person accuses himself, an educated person accuses neither someone else nor himself.

Epictetus

We hope that you have enjoyed this book.

For more editions just like this please search 'Abstract Press'.

ABSTRACT PRESS

Copyright © 2021 by Abstract Press

126